UNFOLD YOURSELF

DR CHETHAN T L

Made with ♥ on the Notion Press Platform
www.notionpress.com

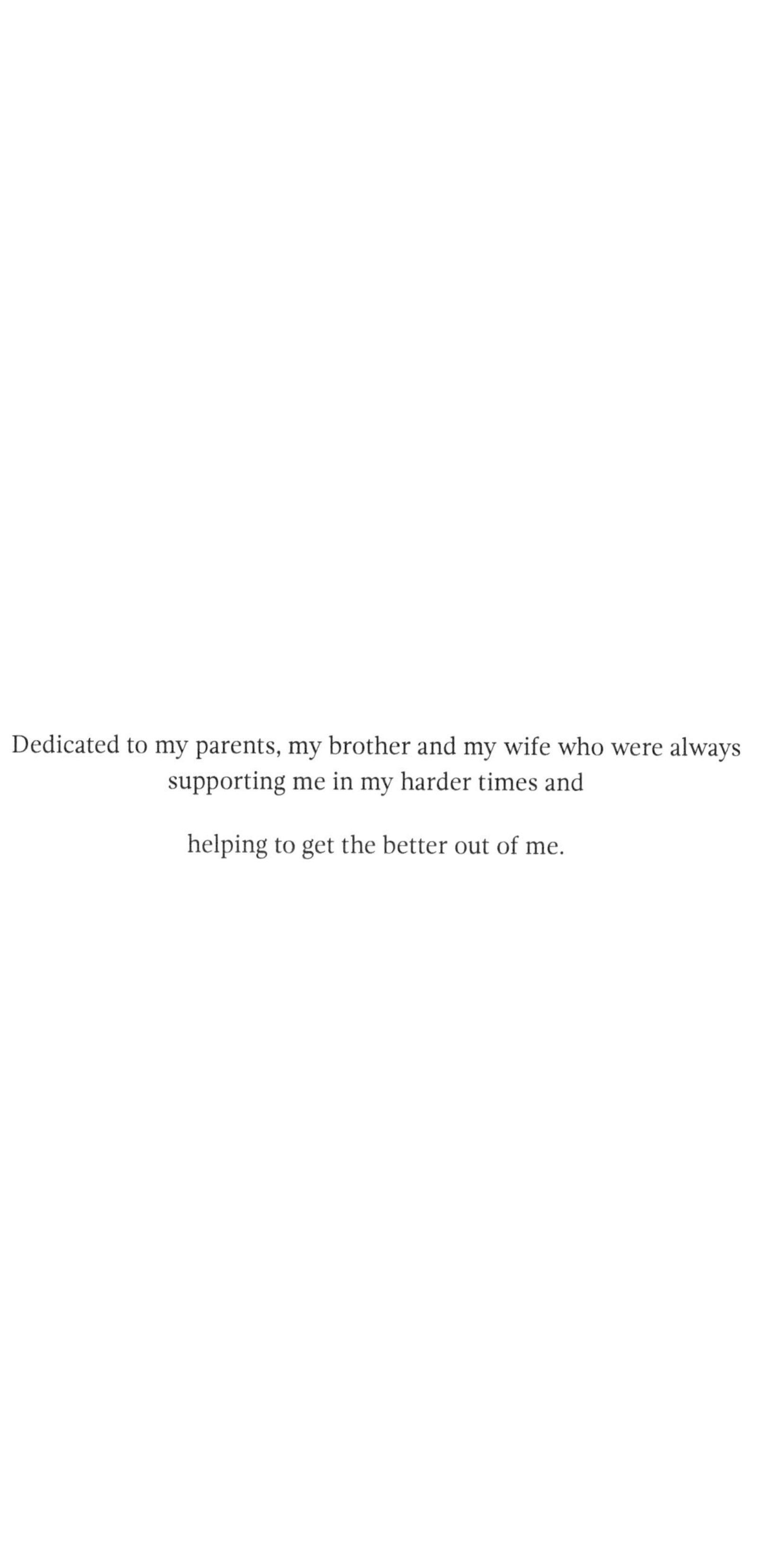

Dedicated to my parents, my brother and my wife who were always supporting me in my harder times and

helping to get the better out of me.

Contents

Foreword

THE BATTLE OF LIFE IS NEVER ENDING ONE. ITS STARTS THE MOMENT WE ARE BORN. ONLY THAT IT HAS DIFFERENT SHADES AND PHASES TO IT WITH NEW TASKS AND GOALS. EVERY ONE HAVE THEIR OWN BATTLE T O FIGHT AND AT THE SAME TIME ALL ARE NOT IN THE SAME BATTLE GROUND.

BUT MANY OF US FAIL IN WINNING BECAUSE THE LACK OF EFFORT OR THE INSECURITIES WE RUN OVER AND OVER ABOUT.

THIS BOOK WITH SMALL LIFE EXPERIENCE OF MINE IS FOR THOSE WARRIORS OF LIFE HAVING SUCH THOUGHTS IN THEM AND HELPING THEM TO OVERCOME AND ACHIEVE THEIR BEST.

ITS ALWAYS SEEM IMPOSSIBLE UNTIL ITS DONE

-NELSON MANDELA.

Prologue

CHAPTER ONE

INTRODUCTION...

The day starts with the worry

The day ends with the worry

What I do next??

Where do I play my next game?

When do I reach my next goal?

When will I make my parents happy?

There is no man in this world I have seen or come across saying that he is not thinking about his future nor he is not worried about his end goals.

Goals are there is to fight, to reach, to score, isn't it??

This is to all the warriors out there fighting against the odds trying to reach the glory of success.

CHAPTER TWO

THE FEAR...

What are u feared of? Feared of defeat??

Feared of losing money??

Losing respect??

Losing yourself??

To start anything new and to start anything big, even for that matter to dream of anything big, we and everyone will be nervous, anxious and at times scared.

Scared for the reason that we don't know the path clearly, thinking about who shines the light in the path, who guides to the end of the dark tunnel, worried about the new beginnings and also worried about the new phase of life of hustle and determination and sacrifice out of your comfort zone.

But one questions always pops out in my mind when ever is see or observe this fear within me. What I am feared of more? Feared of losing the battle or fear of losing itself or fear of losing me itself.

And the answer I always have is fear of losing myself at the end.

Let me put this way, I grew up thinking that I will live my life in a big bungalow with my happy kids and beautiful wife looking and running around, having a pool in my house with all the automated gadgets and hi-tech facility. I imagined my life living in this beautiful house of mine outside the noise and toxicity comfortably lying down on a green lawn facing the sunset sipping a cup of tea. And that is my life I imagined and that is the success for me.

So, if I fear of losing the battle in reaching the success I need stops me from going ahead then I will never be able to reach what I wanted to be and how I wanted to live the life.

Yes, so for me, I fear, I fear of losing myself in not trying to achieve my dreams rather than fear of losing the battle itself.

So, fear is good, fear is good if it drives to be better than your past. Take the leap, jump over the fear and try your best. If u never try, you never know what you could have done some day. Isn't it??

CHAPTER THREE

THE STATE OF MIND...

Worth??

What's my worth?? Am I worthy enough to reach the success I dream of.??

Am I worthy enough to pick the stones to turn them gold in my own hands??

Every human being wants to aspire, wants to dream and wants to live big. Only few of the people doesn't aspire or they give up on what they do.

I wake up every day thinking of creating something big. I wake up every day hoping to make my name glorify in the future. Also, at times these thoughts of glorification also come with doubts of self-confidence and worth fullness isn't it.

What else I can acquire to make it big and large??

What should I do extra to make it such a thing called success.

Everyone has their own capacities and move further.

So the question should be dealt in this way!!

1. Do I have any chance to improve my skills?? If yes, definitely you should go ahead and do it.
2. Do the improvement bring me the success I need? If yes, then go ahead even if its 1% of chances it can be clicked.
3. Should you make any sacrifices before getting those skills?
4. Are these sacrifices worth enough to make?

Let me answer the above two conditions with an example.

I have a fruit vendor near my house, who approximately sells around 20000 worth items in a day and makes a bear minimum profit of 5000 per day. Currently, he wants to grow his business. he wants to be that great fruit vendor whom the whole city applauds for the quality and visits him to buy the products.

So increase his business, he wants to create a bigger enterprise, he wants a bigger stall and more marketing. He has 2 lakh rupees in his account and which he has saved for his daughter's education. Now the big question arises?? Should he sacrifice the money and risk his daughters' education!!!

This is the same diplomatic situation most of the fellow men of ours who are aspiring for success will be going through every day.

Should I risk my education for dance?? Should I risk my house for my new office ?? should I risk my career for my hobby???

The answer is yes and no!! yes only if u believe in yourself and have a right path to go about and no until you find the path. When you want to give up on something what you have to get bigger things , you should carve the path before you walk the path.

The same shop vendor, if he knows what marketing strategy to use to attract customers, knows his limitations and his plus points and also if he can maintain the calm during the storm in initially phases, yes he should definitely go through!!

So is he worth enough to get the success he needs?

Yes, he is, if he knows what he needs to do. What he wants to do and only if he knows what are limitations and capacities. The worthier he is if he reduces his limitations more and en-cash his qualities more.

CHAPTER FOUR

THE UNSEEN PAIN...

My dear brave, yes, it's a highlighted brave!! The pain is unseen, the sufferings you are going through, the battles you are fighting. The struggle which you carry on with a smile. Yes, they are all true. Each and every struggling brave warrior trying to achieve something big will be going through an unseen pain. you me and everyone.

The walls of our house know less those of prayers than our heart chambers.

The pillows have seen more tears than the drenching rain.

The long solo rides we take speak more than the speeches we give.

Isn't it irony that we have lot to share but we won't share. Also, that we want to share, but don't know whom to share.

What is that inhibiting us from going out to the world and expressing your fear, your ideas, your thoughts and your dreams.

It is the term "acceptance". Yes, that is what is letting you not to express yourselves out there.

But have you ever thought that why you need to accepted??

The acceptance is only for the winners, its only for the achievers and its only for the do-ers and not thinkers.

The world will see you as weak if you cry, it will think you as crazy if you explain you dream big. There is no room for talkers here in this practical world. its only for the doers.

Stop crying in silence, rather be string in your silence.

Build yourself in silence.

Plan yourself in silence.

Don't reveal what you want to do until you do.

Don't wait for the hugging supporting shoulder until you are able to support someone else.

As the greats always say, hustle in silence and let the world speak for you later.

CHAPTER FIVE

THE LONELY FISH IN THE SEA...

The next hurdle what we come across is a companion...

Do I have a company to fight this battle??

Will any one support me to get through this quicker stronger

Will anyone help me fight??

Lucky are those who have a companion or a partner to accomplish the journey. A team of two to five friends trying to open up a company. Or a team of two trying to setup a startup.

For that matter, you can also have a strong support system in the form of your wife, your parents or any friends or family. But not always you will have them... so what you gonna do when you don't have any one to get through this.

Half of us don't try to start following our bigger dreams just because we don't have any one to support us to bet through this. Isn't it??

Can I do this alone??

What if I get stuck in between??

Will I have any one to lift me up or give that cushion to push me further??

But you always remember my dear warrior that , whether you are facing an enemy side in the battle field alone or together , you have to finish the battle. Either way if u don't fight, u are gonna be killed.

that's the whole point at end ..

You have to fight... no matter what... whether its only you or a group of fighters. You got to win and finish and fulfill your dreams. Because at the end of the day... it's your life. if you want to live it the way you want... you have to do it with or without anyone.

CHAPTER SIX

THE DARK NIGHTS..

There are so many things we need to manage and withstand even before we start chasing our dreams or during the process.

The family and its responsibilities..

The dips and falls in the journey

The loneliness ..

The fear of losing the battle

The hardships and new comings which you are never used to

The revenge over life inequalities

And the list goes on...

One thing we need to understand is that not all the things you can change or manage. The dips are bound to happen once you have started a new change in life. You would be out of your comfort zone,. You will doing so many new things in life which you would have not done any time before.. these should bring you the teaching lessons in your life Rather than fear. These should the things you should feel more comfortable in dealing with rather than escaping.

Family and its responsibility are something we cant change and we have to get through that.. you need to make lot if sacrifices for the family and in that way only you are going to give your family a better life than before.

Never stop

Never doubt

Jus go ahead and make it large.

CHAPTER SEVEN

THE MEASUREMENT OF SUCCESS...

The measurement of success is different for different people. Isn't it??

Never measure the success in the terms of others and it holds good for failure also.

For a cricketer, success may be to play for nation and be a star or make innumerable records which lives after him. But a simple software engineer, the success would be to be a team lead in the group or CEO of the company. Similarly, for an auto rickshaw guy, success would be to make 10000 Rs per day and able to buy a new auto for himself.

So before you measure your success, define your success, once you are able to define your success, you have put a step in already in achieving it. So before dream big, dream clear, dream the path, dream the result, dream the consequences and dream the way of life.

Conclusion...

THOSE DARK NIGHTS WILL COME DOWN

THE SAD TEARS WILL BE CONVERTED TO HAPPY TEARS

THE LONELINESS WILL BE KILLED

YOU WILL BE FOLLOWED UPON BY PEOPLE KEEPING YOU AS A ROLE MODEL

GO , FIGHT, SUSTAIN, PERSIST, AND MAKE IT LARGE AND BIG AND WIN YOUR DREAMS AND LIVE YOUR LIFE THE WAY YOU IMAGINED ONCE.